POLAR

THE TITANIC BEAR

Illustrations © 1994, 2002 Laurie McGaw
Introduction © 1994, 2002 Leighton H. Coleman III
Text © 1992, 1994, 2002 Leighton H. Coleman III
Jacket, design, and compilation © 1994, 2002 The Madison Press Limited

Little, Brown and Company
Hachette Book Group
237 Park Avenue, New York, NY 10017
Visit our website at www.lb-kids.com
Little, Brown and Company is a division of Hachette Book Group, Inc.
The Little, Brown name and logo are trademarks of Hachette Book Group, Inc.

ISBN 10: 0-316-80909-8
ISBN 13: 978-0-316-80909-2

Library of Congress Catalog Card Number 94-75240

Canadian Cataloguing in Publication Data
 Spedden, Daisy Corning Stone, 1872-1950
    Polar, the Titanic Bear

1. Spedden, Daisy Corning Stone, 1872-1950 — Diaries — Juvenile literature.
2. Titanic (Steamship) — Juvenile literature.
3. Shipwrecks — North Atlantic Ocean — Juvenile literature.
I. McGaw, Laurie. II. Title.

G530.T6S64 1994   j910.91634   C94-931001-8

A CIP catalogue record for this book is available from the British Library.

10 9

DESIGN AND ART DIRECTION
 Gordon Sibley Design Inc.

PRODUCTION DIRECTOR
 Susan Barrable

EDITORIAL DIRECTOR
 Hugh Brewster

PRODUCTION MANAGER
 Sandra L. Hall

PROJECT EDITOR
 Nan Froman

PRINTING AND BINDING
 Oceanic Graphic Printing, Inc.

EDITORIAL ASSISTANCE
 Shelley Tanaka

Madison Press Books
1000 Yonge Street, Suite 303
Toronto, Ontario
Canada M4W 2K2

Printed in China

by Daisy Corning Stone Spedden
Illustrations by Laurie McGaw
Introduction by Leighton H. Coleman III

A MADISON PRESS BOOK
produced for

LITTLE, BROWN AND COMPANY

To the memory of
Douglas and Polar,
and to
Susie and Isabelle,
whose adventures have
just begun

— L.H.C. III

∿

For
Anthony and Gwynne,
with love

— L.M.

Margaretta "Daisy" Spedden
at her home in Tuxedo Park.

INTRODUCTION

I DISCOVERED THIS STORY ABOUT A LITTLE BOY AND his toy bear among the belongings of one of my relatives, Daisy Corning Stone Spedden. It is a true story that Daisy wrote for her only son, Douglas. She painted a cover illustration for it and gave it to Douglas on Christmas Day, in 1913, when he was eight years old.

Douglas (or "Master," as he is called in the story) adored Polar, his beautiful white mohair bear. Polar was made by the famous Steiff company of Germany and was bought by Douglas's aunt at F.A.O. Schwarz in New York City. Now the oldest toy shop in America, F.A.O. Schwarz still sells Steiff bears.

Polar was no ordinary bear. He had several outfits and his own furniture. He took part in all family celebrations and holidays. Best of all, Polar went along on the Spedden family's world travels.

Douglas's parents were very wealthy. They were able to devote their lives to their son, their travels and their hobbies. Daisy kept detailed diaries and was a photography buff. Her husband, Frederic, loved sailing. Douglas had a nanny, Elizabeth Margaret Burns, whom he called "Muddie Boons," because he couldn't quite pronounce her name.

The family lived in a fashionable town outside New York City named Tuxedo Park. They spent summers at the seaside near Bar Harbor, Maine, and winters at resorts around the world. The Speddens traveled on luxurious ocean liners that visited exotic ports in the Caribbean, Africa and the south of France. Douglas was lucky enough to see things that other children only read about, including the Panama Canal, one of the greatest engineering achievements of all time, and the Eiffel Tower, the highest structure in the world in 1912.

But life eighty years ago was not perfect, even for the rich. In those days there was no cure for childhood diseases such as measles, and children who caught the deadly illness had to be separated from other people during the long recovery period. And traveling from Europe to North America was not simply a matter of a six-hour flight on a jet. Planes were rare, and the only way to cross the ocean was to spend seven days on an ocean liner.

When the Speddens were able to book passage to America on the *Titanic*, in April 1912, they considered themselves very lucky. The *Titanic* was the biggest, newest ship in the world — a floating palace that contained every modern convenience and luxury.

Douglas and Polar stepped onto the most magnificent passenger ship ever built in a state of great excitement. They never dreamed that they would soon be part of the most famous sea disaster of all time.

— *Leighton H. Coleman III*

Douglas, with Polar at his feet, sits next to his parents on a hotel balcony in Madeira.

"That's my tenth bear today," said the voice of a young woman proudly. Suddenly I felt myself being hurled through the air, then landing with a thump on a hard wooden bench. I opened my eyes and looked around the large, bright room littered with sawdust, tools and scraps of felt. On either side of a long table sat women who were quickly sewing black glass eyes onto teddy bears. I soon learned that they earned their living by making bears and other stuffed animals for toy shops around the world. Christmas was approaching, and they had been given a large order. This special lot of bears, including me, was to be shipped from Germany to America.

I wondered where America was and how I was to get there, but I didn't have long to wait.

The next morning, I was crammed into a box, my toes touching my ears. Weeks passed in darkness, as I was jostled this way and that. First there was the rumbling of the baggage train, then the swaying of the ship, then the shouts of the dockhands.

But I forgot about my aching limbs when a young woman lifted me out of my box and set me on a shelf with a dozen other bears. She dusted us all off and then tied blue or pink ribbons around our necks. I had arrived at F.A.O. Schwarz, in New York, the largest toy shop in the world.

I was amazed by the beautiful things I could see from my perch. From the ceiling hung every sort of flying machine — airships, aeroplanes and hot-air balloons. In a long case in front of me were little furnishings for dolls' houses — tiny bird cages, baby carriages, and bathtubs with china dolls in them. There was a wonderful railway worked by electricity, and I could see a bright red engine going around and around, past flashing signal towers and stations.

A 1910 postcard of F.A.O. Schwarz's main store.

F. A. O. Schwarz Toy Bazaar
Cor. Fifth Ave. & Thirty-first St.
New York

F.A.O. SCHWARZ,
765 Broadway, bet. 8th & 9th Sts. N.Y.

Mayer, Merkel & Ottmann, Lith. N.Y.

An old advertisement for F.A.O. Schwarz.

Because it was Christmastime, the shop was busy every day. My bear companions disappeared one by one, and I couldn't help wondering when my turn would come.

One day a lady with red cheeks looked me all over carefully, straightened my blue bow, and said she would take me along with her. I was sad to leave my lovely surroundings and hated being packed into a horrid little box again by one of the salesclerks.

For several days I was left in a closet.
I thought everyone had forgotten me, but
finally one morning the lady took me out of the
box. Then we went down to the docks where we
boarded a large ship called the *Caronia*.

Douglas's mother stands with some friends on the deck of the Caronia.

T he decks of the ship were crowded with people saying good-bye. As I looked about wondering what was to become of me, a little boy came running up.

Flinging his arms around the lady with the red cheeks, he cried, "Oh, Aunt Nannie, I wish you were coming with us!"

She gave him a big hug and then presented me to him. The little boy, my new master, had his father and mother with him and Nurse Burns, whom he called "Muddie Boons." Several people came down to see Master's family off, and I was admired by each one in turn, which made me feel very proud.

"How high he holds his head!" Master's father said. "What will you call him?"

"Polar," Master replied promptly.

Reid's Palace Hotel was one of the finest places to stay in Madeira.

Tennis and walks around the harbor were part of a visit to the island.

A week later, we sighted the island of Madeira, near Portugal, which was to be our home for the next few months. It was a beautiful bright afternoon when we went ashore. We traveled through the busy streets to our hotel in a rickety old wooden cart pulled by a bull.

Our hotel was very grand. Master, Muddie Boons and I had a big sunny room overlooking the garden and the blue sea beyond.

I spent many lazy days out under the palms watching Master build little houses with sticks and stones and surround them with miniature gardens. And we rode in the bullock carts whenever we went up into the hills, exploring different parts of the island.

One sad day, Master woke up with red spots all over his face. "He's got measles," the doctor said gravely. "You'll have to put him in quarantine." Everyone looked very worried.

Master, Muddie Boons and I were moved to a little cottage a short distance from the hotel. Master's mother explained that being in "quarantine" meant staying away from the other guests so that we wouldn't give them measles.

We weren't in our new home for five minutes before a big brown mouse scampered across the floor. Poor Muddie Boons shrieked and went after it with a broom. She soon named our cottage "Mouse Castle" because it was full of mice, rats and ants, and she spent all her spare minutes trying to kill them. I didn't like my new quarters a bit, for Master was too sick to even notice me, and I was put in a corner and forgotten.

The doctor visited us often, and every day Master's parents came with fresh eggs and milk. Night after night, I watched as Muddie

"Mouse Castle,"
where Muddie Boons nursed Douglas.

Boons sat awake, holding Master's hot, limp hand in hers. A full week passed, and I began to wonder if he would ever be well enough to play with me again.

But one morning, I heard Master ask for me in a faint little voice. Muddie Boons handed me to him, and he put me on his pillow, and there I lay without stirring the whole day.

Slowly, Master began to grow stronger. He would sit up in bed, wash my face and paws, tie my ribbon and give me my breakfast. I was so happy to see him better that I almost didn't care what he did to me. But I didn't relish the bath Muddie Boons gave me one morning in a horrid, smelly liquid called disinfectant. She gave Master one, too. Then two men came to the garden with a hammock. They carefully lifted Master in as he held tight to his little American flag in one hand and me in the other. Muddie Boons led the way, and we all marched back to our own sunny room in the hotel.

Douglas is carried back to the hotel, where he rests on the balcony.

Soon Douglas is well enough to sit up and play. Here he is photographed with the doctor and with Muddie Boons.

Early in April, we sailed back to America on a ship called the *Adriatic*. After we arrived in New York, we went to Master's new home in Tuxedo Park, which was surrounded by trees and overlooked a little lake.

When the weather turned hot and sticky, we went to the family's summer house near Bar Harbor, Maine. I enjoyed splashing in the ocean with Master or sitting on the rocks while he built forts and castles. Once he forgot about me, and the tide came in and almost carried me out to sea, but luckily Master rescued me just in time.

Polar sits at his own table for Christmas dinner in Tuxedo Park.

When winter came, we returned to Tuxedo Park. Master and I tumbled about in the snow and made snowmen. Best of all he gave me rides on his sled, running as fast as he could across the ice-covered lake while the cold wind whistled in my ears.

At Christmas I had my own tree and new toys to play with. I enjoyed a delicious turkey dinner served on a small table that Master made for me.

Douglas and his
family saw these huge locks
being built for the Panama Canal. The postcard shows
the great amounts of water that had to be controlled.

I n the new year we sailed away to some hot, sunny places. We went to Panama, where a great canal was being built right through the country so that ships could sail from one side to the other. One of the engineers invited Master, Muddie Boons and me to ride out to see it in his big private car. Bright flocks of parrots flew from the trees as we roared down the jungle roads.

Bermuda was our last stop. Master took me to a beautiful beach where we

Douglas and his mother on the beach in Bermuda.

spent many a long afternoon. He would make a sort of throne out of sand for me to sit on and say, "Now, Polar, don't you run away, but just stay quiet while I work."

So I sat there watching him play and sniffing the salt air.

The next winter we once more set sail on the *Caronia*, this time for Algiers, in northern Africa. The weather was sunny, so we spent our days on deck romping about with the other children. The captain and Master were great friends, and we were often invited to his room for a cup of "tea," as Master called his hot water and sugar.

In Algiers we saw Arabs dressed in long flowing robes. We stayed in a big hotel with a garden, where I would sit on a bench with Muddie Boons while Master played ball.

In February we celebrated George Washington's birthday. Master invited a few friends. We decorated the table with American flags, and Master dressed in red, white and blue. After our tea party we all fished presents from a big bag!

A postcard showing the main square in Algiers.

Douglas and his father in the hotel garden.

752. - MONTE-CARLO. - Place du Casino - Café de Paris
Casino Place - Coffee-house

11 CANNES. - LES PALMIERS DE LA CROISETTE ET LE MONT CHEVALIER.

These postcards show scenes of Monte Carlo and Cannes in 1912.

From Algiers we set sail for the south coast of France. At Monte Carlo, we rode to our hotel on the hill in a funny narrow railway. Master told me it was a funicular railway and that it was pulled along by a cable.

Then we went to Cannes where we stayed for nearly a month. I sat in the hotel garden every morning while Master had an hour's spelling lesson with Muddie Boons.

One day we heard a loud buzzing noise.

"An aeroplane!" Master shouted, throwing down his books.

"Goodness me!" Muddie Boons cried, jumping to her feet. We all craned our necks up to the sky and watched as the aeroplane circled overhead. I could see the pilot sitting in the cockpit with his goggles on, and he waved at us before heading out over the sea.

e took the night train to Paris. Strolling in the Tuileries Gardens, we saw boys sailing their boats in the fountains and watched hot-air balloons rising toward the sky. Master took me partway up the Eiffel Tower one day and told me it was 984 feet high. He was always telling me the height and length of things.

I was sorry when it was time to go back to America, for I loved Paris. But Master was excited because we were to sail to New York on the *Titanic*, a magnificent new ship. Everyone said she was the biggest ship in the world. We were going to be on her very first voyage. The *Titanic* had left England

A postcard of the Titanic *and one of the ship's diamond-shaped luggage stickers.*

WHITE STAR LINE

NAME_____ ROOM_____
BOOKED TO_____ VIA_____
STEAMER_____ SAILING_____
FULL FOREIGN ADDRESS_____

J-3487

WANTED
FIRST
CLASS

The Nomadic *carried Douglas and his family out to the* Titanic.

the day before and her first stop was at Cherbourg, France. We took a train to Cherbourg and that evening went out to the huge ship on a little tugboat.

As we stepped on board, the ship's doctor, who had known all of us on the *Adriatic*, kissed Master and said, "I see you still have Polar with you, little man!"

We had fairly smooth weather those first few days and spent most of our time on deck, where Master would spin his whip top or play ball. But we also loved exploring the great ship. There was a giant staircase with a big glass dome over it.

Trying out the rowing machine and the mechanical camel in the ship's gymnasium.

The Grand Staircase.

Master sent me flying down the banister one morning. In the ship's gymnasium, we saw bicycles and rowing machines and even a mechanical camel for the passengers to ride on.

There was a lovely sun parlor on the upper deck where we spent our afternoons, and Master allowed a little girlfriend of his to play with me. We ate in the first-class dining saloon. The tables there were covered with stiffly starched white tablecloths and polished silver, and the ship's band played for us every night. And our stateroom was even bigger than Master's bedroom at home!

One day Master's mother and Muddie Boons went down to the lower decks and had a Turkish bath. They didn't like this hot steam bath one bit, although they did enjoy a cooling dip in the ship's swimming pool afterwards.

No. 659

WHITE STAR LINE.

R.M.S. "TITANIC."

This ticket entitles bearer to use of Turkish or Electric Bath on one occasion.

Paid 4/= or 1 Dollar.

It was our fifth night at sea. I had been in bed a few hours when I suddenly opened my eyes. The lights had been turned on. Muddie Boons was dressing Master in a great hurry.

After a Turkish steam bath, passengers could cool off in the elegant room shown above or jump into the Titanic's swimming pool.

"Come, we're taking a trip to see the stars," she said. Master's parents were already dressed. They were gathering a few belongings together. I was surprised when I saw Master's mother reach for lifebelts. Then, seizing me from my little net rack beside Master's bed, she tucked me under his arm. We soon joined a group of people standing in the main hall.

Everyone was very quiet, talking in hushed voices. Someone whispered that we had struck an iceberg and that water was pouring into the ship. A young man in uniform helped fasten on Master's lifebelt. Patting him on the head, he said, "Good-bye, little man."

Then Master's father told us to follow him to the top deck, where we would climb into one of the lifeboats.

The lifeboat was swinging out from the ship's side, and people had difficulty climbing aboard. Our little party kept together, and when there were about forty of us in the boat, an officer cried, "Lower away," and we were let down to the water in awful jerks. Master clasped me in his arms. His eyes were shut tight, and his face was white. We finally reached the water safely and rowed off toward a faint light on the horizon.

It was very dark. Aside from the stars and the brilliantly lighted ship that towered above us, we could see nothing. Soon after we left the *Titanic*, the captain sent up rockets as a distress signal.

We all watched the ship steadily, except Master, who was asleep. Two hours later, we saw the last light go out and heard the dreadful cries that told us all was over. The great *Titanic* had gone down.

It seemed like a horrible dream. The heartbreaking silence and feeling of utter loneliness cast a deep gloom over our little boatload.

Toward three o'clock in the morning, an icy breeze sprang up and the sea grew rough. Master opened his eyes and said he felt seasick. But Muddie Boons, who had him on her lap, soon quieted him with a story of Cinderella.

About an hour later, someone suddenly shouted, "Here comes a ship!" Looking toward the horizon, we first saw a white light and then some rockets.

As the ship gradually approached, we feared she might either run us down or not see us at all, since we had no lantern. But soon she slowed down and then stopped.

As the faint mist cleared just before dawn, the new moon was setting, and a star was faintly twinkling on the pink horizon. The first rays of the sun cast a wonderful glow on the icebergs that rose from the ocean all around us.

Master suddenly opened his eyes and looking about him exclaimed, "Oh, Muddie, look at the beautiful North Pole with no Santa Claus on it."

A woman who had been crying smiled at him through her tears.

Our rescue ship, the *Carpathia*, looked very small amidst the few bits of wreckage where the huge *Titanic* had gone down. We finally drew alongside, and the men climbed aboard the *Carpathia* on rope ladders. The women were hauled up in a sort of swing, and the children in canvas bags.

The Carpathia *raced through the night to rescue the* Titanic's *passengers in the lifeboats.*

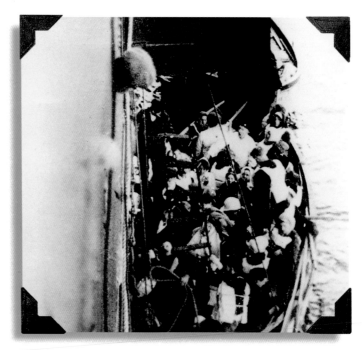

Soon everyone had been rescued — except for me. I lay alone in the empty lifeboat. Several minutes went by, but nothing happened. Everyone seemed to have forgotten me. My heart began to pound. I imagined being left there, tossed by the waves forever. Would I ever see Master again?

Suddenly I felt a terrible jerk, and then another. The boat swayed dangerously. I nearly fell into the icy water as several sailors pulled the lifeboat up to the decks of the *Carpathia*. I slid down the ribs of the boat, banging my back against each one along the way, and landed in a puddle.

"That's the last of them, then," said a sailor. He turned the boat over with a bang, and I fell onto the hard deck in a wet, miserable heap.

I lay there for what must have been hours. Then I heard a kind voice.

"Hello, there! Fancy seeing you again."

It was one of the sailors from the *Titanic*. He picked me up and squeezed the water out of me, quite taking my breath away. Then he carried me down some stairs and into a warm room. It was full of passengers with blankets around them. Many of them held hot drinks.

Sailors hoist one of the lifeboats aboard the Carpathia, *while Titanic survivors line up for a hot meal.*

Form No. 1—100.—2.2.09.

The Marconi International Marine Communication Company, Ltd.

WATERGATE HOUSE, YORK BUILDINGS, ADELPHI, LONDON, W.C.

Sent date 18th Apl 12.

OFFICE .... 18 Apl. 12 .... 19 ____

CHARGES TO PAY.

No. 105/100 .... Words 8

Prefix ....

Code ....

Office of Origin ....

Service Instructions : ....

Marconi Charge	...	
Other Line Charge	...	
Delivery Charge	...	
Total		
Office sent to	Time sent	By whom sent
	6.35 m.	

READ THE CONDITIONS PRINTED ON THE BACK OF THE FORM.

To : Kerneys— Cromwell, Conn.

all safe notify family + friends Spedden

CONINGHAM BROS., Printers, etc., Limehouse, E.

PLEASE ASK FOR OFFICIAL RECEIPT.

Douglas's father sent this telegram from the rescue ship to relatives at home.

"Polar!" a familiar voice shouted from across the room. It was Master. He rushed over and took me in his arms. I was delighted to see him again, too. But I was also rather upset to see that he was holding an ugly little brown bear. His mother had bought it for him in the ship's barbershop, thinking I had fallen overboard! As soon as Master saw me, however, he hugged and kissed me. He took me to bed with him that night and every night after, forgetting all about the other bear.

Survivors make clothes from blankets and comfort one another on the Carpathia.

During the next four long days, Master and I spent as much time as we could on deck, even though it was rainy or foggy every day. But the ship was so crowded, with more than seven hundred *Titanic* survivors as well as the *Carpathia*'s passengers, that there was hardly room to move. Master's mother and Muddie Boons spent hours cutting up blankets to make clothes for people who had none.

A three-year-old boy wears a nightgown made from one of the blankets.

At last we slowly steamed up New York Harbor in the middle of a thunderstorm. We were escorted by several boats full of people taking flash pictures of us.

"Look at the big parade, Muddie Boons, with no brass band!" Master cried as we saw the huge crowds of people and cars lining the docks. We were glad to escape the hubbub with members of the family who had come down to meet us.

I was happy to settle down to quiet country life in Tuxedo Park. The experience we had gone through seemed to bring Master and me closer together than ever before. He made a great pet of me and supplied me with two new suits of clothes and a little white wooden bed. I often thought back to how I was almost lost on the wide ocean. But I felt much better when Master tucked me beside him in bed each night and whispered softly in my ear, "Good night, Polar."

Master goes to school now, and I am left alone much of the time. But I always look forward to the warm greeting he gives me on his return. He has been a good Master, and I hope he will be blessed with a long and happy life. Though I realize that I shall see less and less of him as the years go by, I shall always feel, no matter what happens, that I occupy a large corner of his true and tender heart and that he will be loyal to me till the end. ❧

EPILOGUE

The letters, diaries, photo albums and mementoes of Daisy Spedden record a way of life that is gone forever. Her family trunk is a time capsule from another world. Turning the pages of Daisy's photo albums, one sees pictures of large houses with beautiful gardens, where elegantly dressed people attended parties. In the winter they boarded ocean liners to stay at grand hotels in places like Cannes, Madeira and Bermuda. No one had to work to make a living except the servants who took care of the children and the housework. Few of the small number of people who lived this way eighty years ago seemed to have thought their comfortable world would ever come to an end.

Daisy and her stepmother visit the home
of relatives in Connecticut.

54

Muddie Boons with Douglas and his mother in 1909.

Daisy looks on as her son and his grandmother
fish in the garden pond.

In the family's newly acquired automobile.

Douglas poses in his cowboy outfit in his
grandmother's garden.

The Speddens' photo albums show that Douglas, their only child, was the focus of their life. Many of Daisy's photographs show him surrounded by beautifully made toys — it was the golden age of toys when new creations such as teddy bears and electric train sets came into being. Dressing up in costumes was also popular, and the albums

A painting of Douglas in his sailor suit.

include photos of Douglas in a cowboy outfit and in a Japanese kimono holding a parasol. His nurse, Elizabeth Margaret Burns, nicknamed Muddie Boons, is often pictured with him since she accompanied Douglas and his parents on all their trips.

At the end of one European holiday, the Speddens took a train from Paris to Cherbourg on the morning of Wednesday, April 10, 1912. Also on the train were other well-to-do Americans including John Jacob Astor, whom the newspapers called the world's richest man. In Cherbourg that evening, the Speddens, the

Polar, and other bears like him, were made by the world renowned Margarete Steiff company of Germany from 1909 to 1929. These bears had white mohair coats, black glass eyes, stitched noses and moveable joints (above). International demand for Steiff toys with their "Button-in-Ear" trademark (top) grew rapidly in the early 1900s. Teddy bears, such as this gold mohair plush bear from the 1920s (left), were especially popular.
The Steiff company has an almost legendary reputation in the world of toys and is still considered to be the foremost teddy bear manufacturer in the world.

The Nomadic, *which once ferried the* Speddens *out to the* Titanic *from Cherbourg (opposite), is now a restaurant on the Seine in Paris. Some of the original interiors of this only surviving White Star ship still remain.*

The only photograph of the Speddens on the Titanic *shows Douglas spinning his top on the deck (below).*

Astors and other New York bound passengers took a small boat, the *Nomadic*, out to the huge *Titanic* which had just arrived from Southampton, England. Then the ship left for Queenstown, Ireland, its last stop before crossing the Atlantic.

In her diary, Daisy Spedden records the pleasant shipboard routine on board the luxurious new liner. What the Speddens didn't know was that on Sunday, April 14,

the *Titanic*'s radio operators received seven ice warnings. At 11:40 p.m. that night, the ship's lookouts spotted a large iceberg dead ahead. The iceberg struck the starboard side of the *Titanic*'s bow, and water began to pour into the lower decks of the ship.

Daisy and her husband, Frederic, were awakened by *"a sudden shock, a grinding*

noise and a stopping of the ship's engines." They immediately got dressed and went up on deck, where they were told what had happened. Daisy wrote that it was too dark to see anything except some ice on the forward deck. But she noticed that the ship was already tilting, and so she and Frederic hurried downstairs to awaken Douglas, Muddie Boons and Daisy's maid.

At midnight, the captain ordered the radio operators to call to other ships for help. Minutes later, the crew began to load passengers into the lifeboats. There were only sixteen lifeboats and four collapsible boats on the ship — room for only half of the more than 2,200 passengers on board.

An hour later, crewmen helped Daisy, Douglas, Muddie Boons and Daisy's maid into lifeboat No. 3. Then, since there seemed to be no more women and children on deck, about twenty men, including Frederic, were allowed to jump in. The boat was lowered 65 feet to the ocean surface. It was so dark that no one could find a lantern. But until dawn, the survivors in lifeboat No. 3

managed to keep track of the other lifeboats from the ship by following the gleam of their lanterns across the water.

Just after 2 a.m., the last lifeboat left the *Titanic*. There were more than 1,500 people still on board the steeply tilting ship. Minutes later the bow plunged under the water and passengers began to jump overboard. Then the forward funnel collapsed.

The *Titanic's* lights went out for good. The stern tilted high into the air, and then the ship broke in two before it slid beneath the waves. The passengers in lifeboat No. 3 couldn't persuade the sailor steering the boat to go back and try to rescue people in the water. He was afraid that their small boat would be drawn underwater by the suction created by the huge *Titanic*.

Just before dawn, the chilled survivors in the lifeboats spied the lights of an approaching steamer. After boarding the rescue ship, the *Carpathia*, Daisy Spedden wrote to a friend in Madeira describing the ordeal they had been through. One passage reveals, with refreshing honesty, what she felt after spending a long, cold, fearful night in the cramped lifeboat:

One fat woman in our boat had been dreadful all along for she never stopped talking and telling the sailors what to do, and she imbibed from her brandy flask frequently, never offering a drop to anyone else. It was very cold, too, just before dawn, when a breeze came up and a chilly blast from the iceberg struck us. As we approached the ship "our woman" promptly sprang up in order to get off first, when she had been warned to sit still, and it gave me the greatest satisfaction to grab her by her lifebelt and drag her down.

She fell flat in the bottom of the boat with her heels in the air and was furious because we held her there till we were alongside the Carpathia *when we were all charmed to let her go up in the sling first.*

IN THE TRYING DAYS THAT FOLLOWED THE DISASTER, THE Speddens worked hard to relieve the suffering of those aboard the *Carpathia*. Their efforts won them the admiration and friendship of that ship's captain, Arthur Rostron. Daisy and Frederic Spedden were remembered by their fellow survivors for their many kindnesses, and Daisy records in her diary entry for April 15 that she went to bed "*worn out both mentally and physically*" after "*working all day looking after the people, our special protégés, besides some steerage passengers.*" To her friend in Madeira she wrote that "*we spend our time sitting on people who are*

For years Daisy recorded daily events and descriptions of her travels in her diary.

Douglas and Polar, Christmas 1912.

Nine-year-old Douglas in his bedroom with Polar.

cruel enough to say that no steerage should have been saved, as if they weren't human beings!"

But the world would soon ask the opposite question, demanding why so few people from third class had been rescued, and a popular song about the *Titanic* would claim that "they kept them down below where they were the first to go."

Historians now point to the *Titanic* disaster, which was followed two years later by World War I, as the beginning of the end of an era where society was sharply divided between rich and poor.

After the *Titanic* tragedy the Speddens carried on with their busy lives and travels much as before, but as Daisy wrote, "*all the values of [our] life changed, and the daily incidents, which once seemed of such importance to us, dwindled into mere trivialities.*"

Sadly, the *Titanic* disaster was but a foreshadowing of deeper pain to come to the Speddens. Just three years after the sinking of the ship, nine-year-old Douglas was killed in a car accident near the family's summer camp in Maine. It was one of the first automobile accidents in the state. No one knows what happened to Polar the bear.

Wee Wah Lodge, the Speddens' home in Tuxedo Park.

Daisy Spedden, who had kept such meticulous records of all the events in her life, stopped writing her diaries at the time of her child's death. But her photograph albums continued, showing Daisy in black mourning dress and Frederic with mourning bands.

The Speddens had no other children and spent the rest of their lives among close friends and family or traveling. Every winter, after enjoying a few weeks in New York City, they traveled abroad. Returning home each spring, they divided their time between Tuxedo Park and their summer home in Maine. They both lived long lives and died just a few years apart — Frederic in 1947 and Daisy in 1950.

Perhaps the words Daisy wrote in her school alumni magazine, for the young women graduating in the class of 1933, best show how she remained determined to focus on her good fortune throughout her life:

As my mind reverts to the past, filled with the lights,
as well as the deep shadows that come to so many of us,
my fervent wish is that the memories of your life
and your friendships may be as happy as mine....

ACKNOWLEDGEMENTS

Laurie McGaw would like to extend special thanks to Anthony Facciolo, who posed as the model for Douglas, and to her friend Sue Teeter, Anthony's mother. Thanks also to the following who posed as models for the illustrations: Ross Phillips, Gwynne Phillips, Patricia Moon Bartman (who also contributed her organizational skills), Deborah Gee, Norm Gee, Jennifer Gee, Cynthia J. Apitius, Kim Phillips, Gail Reddick, Scott Horner and Kevin Hancey. Thanks to Carol McGaw, Kathleen Phillips, George's Trains (Toronto), The Little Dollhouse Company (Toronto), Martin House Dolls and Toys (Thornhill, Ontario) and Moon Shadow Antiques (Badjeros, Ontario) for props; Deborah Gee, Cynthia J. Apitius and Hollywood Costumes (Thornhill, Ontario) for costumes; and Pat Billard for sewing Polar's outfits.

Leighton H. Coleman III would like to remember his grandparents, Mr. and Mrs. Leighton H. Coleman Esq., who had the foresight to preserve family treasures for the next generation. Thanks to Merri Ferrell for all her invaluable advice and assistance, and to Don Dirks for his tireless help. And, finally, thanks to Josh and Julie McClure of Island Color Photography for the wonderful reproductions of the archival photographs.

Madison Press Books would like to extend special thanks to Ken Marschall for his expert technical advice and inspiration in the creation of the *Titanic* paintings. We would also like to thank Don Lynch for his historical expertise. We are grateful to all those who have let us use their photographs: George Behe, Joe Carvalho, Jürgen Cieslik, Mr. George A. Fenwick, Mrs. B. Hambly, Otmar Dreher and Jörg Junginger of Margarete Steiff GmbH, Ed and Karen Kamuda of the Titanic Historical Society (P.O. Box 51053, Indian Orchard, Massachusetts 01151-0053), Don Lynch and Ken Marschall. And, finally, thanks to Dick Frantz, who identified Polar as a Steiff bear.

PICTURE CREDITS

All photographs are from the albums of Daisy Corning Stone Spedden unless otherwise stated.

Front flap: (Top right) Ken Marschall Collection
Back flap: Illustration by Daisy Corning Stone Spedden
Back cover: (Left) Ken Marschall Collection

6: Illustration by Daisy Corning Stone Spedden

12: (Left) Collection of The New-York Historical Society (Right) The New York Public Library

14: (Top) Kamuda Collection/The Titanic Historical Society

24: (Top right) Mary Evans Picture Library

26: (Left) Mary Evans Picture Library

28: Mary Evans Picture Library

32: Ken Marschall Collection

34: (Top left) The Father Browne S.J. Collection (Top right) Joe Carvalho Collection (Bottom) Ken Marschall Collection

37: (Left) George Behe Collection (Top right) Brown Brothers (Bottom) Ken Marschall Collection

44: (Top) Ken Marschall Collection (Bottom left) Ken Marschall Collection (Bottom right) Brown Brothers

47: (Left) Courtesy of Mr. George A. Fenwick (Right) The Titanic Historical Society

48: Spedden family archives / J. Aidan Booth

50: (Top left) Mary Evans Picture Library (Top right) Mary Evans Picture Library (Bottom) Mrs. B. Hambly Collection

57: (Top right) Margarete Steiff GmbH (Middle right) Jürgen Cieslik of Verlag Marianne Cieslik (Bottom) With permission of Kunstverlag Weingarten/Germany from R. and C. Pistorius: Die schönsten Teddys und Tiere von Steiff.

58: (Top and inset) Ken Marschall Collection (Bottom) The Father Browne S.J. Collection

59: Painting by Ken Marschall